Stock Returns and Option Prices.
A Simulation Analysis

Martin Georg Haas

Bibliographic information published by the German National Library:

The German National Library lists this publication in the National Bibliography; detailed bibliographic data are available on the Internet at http://dnb.dnb.de.

ISBN: 9783346474872
This book is also available as an ebook.

© GRIN Publishing GmbH
Nymphenburger Straße 86
80636 München

Print and binding: Books on Demand GmbH, Norderstedt, Germany
Printed on acid-free paper from responsible sources.

The present work has been carefully prepared. Nevertheless, authors and publishers do not incur liability for the correctness of information, notes, links and advice as well as any printing errors.

GRIN web shop: https://www.grin.com/document/1043527

Zeppelin University

Corporate Management and Economics

Stock Returns and Option Prices

Assignment

in

Advanced Finance

Submitted by:	Martin Haas
Programme:	Corporate Management and Economics
Date:	15.06.2018

Contents

List of Tables

List of Figures

1 Introduction

When Thales of Miletus in the 6th century B.C. secured himself the right to rent the citys olive presses for a fixed price one year in advance, he may have established the first futures contract in human history. Anticipating an upcoming olive harvest that would greatly surpass the years before, he now was able to buy (rent) low and sell high, when his prediction was correct. The time came around, and the olive harvest was, as foreseen, a great one, making him a rich man. Although anecdotal, this story captures the essence of a common derivative: the forward/future contract. Besides being an interesting object of speculative investing, its technical use is to hedge ones position against the risk of large changes in the value of the underlying asset, by agreeing with the option issuer to a future trade with a fixed price. When the execution of this trade is only *optional*, the contract is called option.

The option seems obviously to be the better contract, because it forgoes the obligation to exercise when the market situation is unfavourable. Nevertheless, significantly more futures contracts are traded worldwide, with 14.48 billion future and 10.36 billion option contracts in 2017 (Futures Industries Association 2018). Reasons for the relative popularity of futures, according to Picardo (2018) from Investopedia, are the better suit for trading certain commodities such as currencies and indexes, the fixed upfront trading cost, higher liquidity, the fact that they exhibit no time decay and the easier pricing compared to options. In this paper, the pricing is of interest.

The price of a future contract can be determined by the current commodity price and the costs of carrying the commodity until the maturity of the contract. The price of an option contract is, generally, determined by the payoff of the option plus a part that prices the risk of the value change of the underlying asset, which are also referred to as the intrinsic and the time value. The valuation of the time value of an option is much more complicated than the valuation of the cost of carry and because of this a huge topic of academic research.

Theoretically, the option value is the discounted future payoff of the option, with the difficulty that the future price of the underlying asset is unknown and needs to be estimated. The determination of the distribution of future asset prices is one of the critical assumptions in this calculation. Black and Scholes (1972) used the assumption of lognormally distributed returns with constant volatility in their famous option pricing formula. Although these assumptions seem questionable in the face of volatility clustering and the fact that stock returns are not distributed lognormally (see e.g. Johnson, Zuber, and Gandar (2007), Beckers (1981)), we can take away the fact that stock returns and their volatility are key inputs to option pricing. Conversely, options can be used to estimate the expected volatility of the underlying stocks, a concept which is called implied volatility (Latane and Rendleman 1976). An intuitive and simplified explanation for this method is to input option prices into the Black&Scholes formula and solving for the standard deviation.

Option pricing is also influenced due to structure and institutions of the market, e.g. by information asymmetries between Market participants both in the option and the stock markets (Bali and Hovakimian 2009; Lin and Lu 2015; Pan and Poteshman 2006). Although the debate over which market leads the price-finding process is not settled, the literature finds evidence for informed traders preferring either the stock or the option market, leading to prices that deviate from theoretical prices. (Cao and Han 2013) find a negative effect on option returns when options are less liquid and the option open interests are higher, which they find "consistent with option dealers charging a higher option premium when the options are more difficult to hedge and option demands are higher". Gurdip Bakshi and Chen (2000) find that market micro-structure effects such as bid-ask spreads, tick size restriction etc. can explain why option prices do not change, or do not change as expected with changes in the price of the underlying asset (e.g call prices decreasing in face of face of rising underlying price).

This paper is concerned with analysing the basic determinants of option prices. As described above, these are the informations derived from the underlying stock, namely the mean and the volatility of its returns. Therefore, this paper aims at answering the question, what influence stock return mean and volatility have on the respective option prices. This can be important to option traders trying to identify the stocks for which to trade options, by providing an understanding for the foundations of the option pricing and the information those prices provide. To isolate these basic determinants from the other influences, described above as structural and institutional factors, a simulation study is conducted. Section 2 will provide the theoretical framework and simulation methodology for the study. Section 3 describes the used dataset and section 4 presents and discusses the results of the simulation.

2 Theoretical Framework and Simulation Methodology

In order to analyse the relationship of stock returns and their respective option prices, a quasi-simulation that is based on a real stock sample will be conducted. The following sections describe the basic mathematical concepts of the simulation and the practical implementation of the simulation.

2.1 Stock Price Simulation

To determine the payoff of an option, the price of the underlying stock at maturity S_{t+m} has to be determined. The price of a stock at a given time can be constructed as the sum of the consecutive returns of the stock up until the given time, if the starting price is known. Following this approach, the stock price at maturity will be calculated as

$$S_{t+m} = S_t + \sum_{j=1}^{m} r_{t+m}\sigma + \mu m \mu_r, \tag{1}$$

where r_t denotes the stock return at time t given by $S_t - S_{t-1}$, m denotes the time to maturity and μ_r denotes the mean of the stock returns. The parameters σ and μ are used to vary the volatility and the mean of the returns in the simulation. This allows to analyse the relationship between the stock returns and the respective option prices under ceteris paribus conditions.

2.2 Option Price Calculation

Options will be considered from the perspective of the buyer ("long position"), who acquires the right to buy ("call") or to sell the underlying asset ("put"). The price of a put option at time t will be denoted as P_t, and of a call option as C_t respectively. The time to maturity in days, i.e. the time left until the option expires, will be denoted as m. The interest rate used for discounting, the risk-free-rate, is denoted by i. The strike price, i.e. the price at which the underlying asset can be traded if the option is exercised, will be denoted as K, the price of the underlying stock at time t as S_t. Only european options, which can only be executed at the expiry date will be considered. As such, the price of an option is calculated as discounted payoff at maturity according to:

$$P_t = \frac{P_{t+m}}{(1+i)^{\frac{m}{365}}} = \frac{max(K - S_{t+m}, 0)}{(1+i)^{\frac{m}{365}}} = \frac{(K - S_{t+m})^+}{(1+i)^{\frac{m}{365}}} \tag{2}$$

for put options and

$$C_t = \frac{C_{t+m}}{(1+i)^{\frac{m}{365}}} = \frac{max(S_{t+m} - K, 0)}{(1+i)^{\frac{m}{365}}} = \frac{(S_{t+m} - K)^+}{(1+i)^{\frac{m}{365}}} \tag{3}$$

for call options. Here $(\cdot)^+$ denotes the option payoff at maturity.

2.3 Simulation Implementation

In the simulation, 1000 stock prices for a standard maturity of 90 days (≈ 3 months) will be calculated by drawing 90 random values from the stock returns and plugging them into equation 1, with a starting price S_1 of 100. These simulated prices build the stock price distribution at maturity used for the option pricing. They don't rely on any distributional assumptions as in e.g. the Black&Scholes model, only on the characteristics of the used stock sample and that all outcomes are equally likely.

For each stock, the call and put option prices get calculated for strike prices K ranging from 0 to 200 by 0.5 increments. An option price for a certain strike price is calculated as the mean of the 1000 option prices, calculated by equation 2 (puts) or (3) (calls) respectively. A fixed risk-free-rate of 10% is used.

By looking at the correlation of return mean and standard deviation with the simulated option prices for a sample of different stocks, an analysis of the relationship of stock returns and option prices will be conducted. By varying the volatility and mean parameters (σ, μ) the influence of a change in stock return mean and volatility on option prices will be assessed.

2.4 Hypotheses

For an increase in mean of the returns, i.e that the stock becomes more profitable, the payoff of call option rises monotonically, whereas the payoff of put options decreases monotonically. This is obvious, since the call payoff is calculated by subtracting the strike price from the stock price at maturity and higher returns will lead to higher stock prices. The opposite is true for puts. Therefore, the first hypothesis states that:

> **H1:** Stocks with higher return means exhibit higher call and lower put option prices. An increase in mean return ceteris paribus leads to an increase in call prices and a decrease in put prices

Higher volatility of stock returns indicates larger price movements, meaning a higher volatility of stock prices. If the prices are distributed symmetrically, and the strike price equals the mean price at maturity, an increase in the volatility of the returns leads to a larger range of possible option payoffs. This is indicated schematically in figure 1. Taking the average over all strike prices, an increase in return volatility should lead to an increase of option prices and vice versa. Therefore, the second hypothesis states:

> **H2:** Stocks with higher return volatility exhibit higher call and put option prices. An increase in return volatility ceteris paribus leads to an increase in call prices and put prices

Figure 1: Schematic option payoffs for different stock volatilites under symmetric price distribution

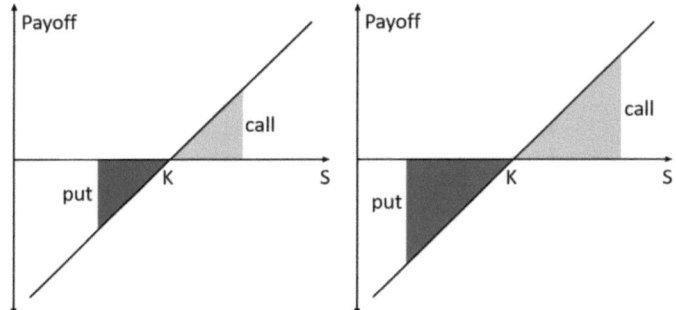

(a) Call and put payoff for low volatility (b) Call and put payoff for high volatility

3   Data

The sample of stocks consists of the constituents of the S&P500 index, with daily adjusted prices of the last 10 years (2008-06-01 to 2018-06-01). The data is downloaded from Yahoo

Finance via the R-Package Quantmod. Stocks with missing values and incomplete time series were discarded, leaving 448 stocks in the sample. The full summary statistics for the returns of these stocks are presented in table 5 in the appendix.

On average, the sampled stocks returns have a positive mean of 0.03, with a range from -0.2 to 0.62 (see table 1 and figure 2). With returns of 0.62 (Amazon, AMZN) and 0.32 (Google, both GOOGL and GOOG) This and the stock returns average skew of -0.39 indicate that the sampled returns tend to be positive, which is not unreasonable for the top 500 stocks of the United States. For this simulation it indicates that the simulated prices are expected to increase on average, from which follows that the prices of calls should be higher than those of puts. As the return distribution is asymmetric and right-skewed, increasing volatility in the simulation will tend to produce higher call prices and lower put prices, or at least lead to a lower price increase than for calls.

In order to get reliable evidence for the skewness of the returns, D'Agostinos test of skewness is performed for each stock return sample. At a significance level of 5% it finds 88.4% of the stock returns to be skewed. Overall, 72.5% of stock returns are identified as negatively, and 15.8% as positively skewed.

The volatility of the stocks returns, measured by the standard deviation, shows a large range. Looking at figure 2 we can see that this is due to some stocks with extreme volatility, namely Amazon (AMZN, 9.26), Google (both GOOGL, 8.16 and GOOG, 8.05), Chipotle Mexican Grill (CMG, 7.86) and AutoZone (AZO, 6.62) . On average the standard deviations are centered around 1.04. From this, option prices can be expected to exhibit some extreme values for some stocks, e.g. the stocks named above.

Table 1: Summary statistics of the sampled stock returns

	return mean	return std. deviation	return skew
min	-0.2	0.16	-10.22
max	0.62	9.26	18.84
mean	0.03	1.08	-0.39
std. deviation	0.05	1.04	1.57
skewness	5.83	4.27	3.47

4 Results

4.1 Simulated Stock Prices

The simulated stock prices behave according to the stated hypotheses. On average, prices increased by 2.72% (from a starting value of 100) in scenario 1, where no parameters were changed (compare table 2). Increasing or decreasing the mean of the returns by 10% (scenario 4) changes the growth in price accordingly. So far only the functioning of the simulation according to the specified formula for price simulation has been confirmed.

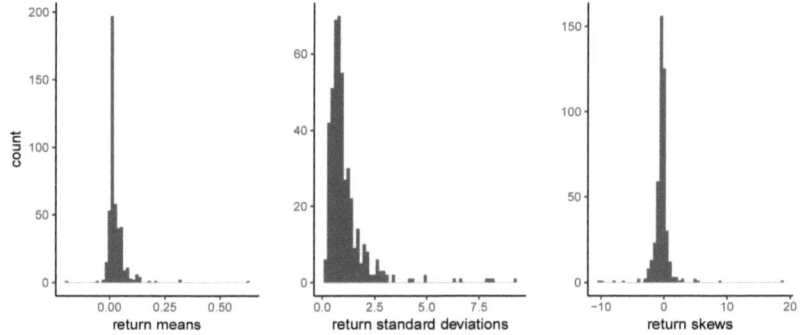

Figure 2: Histogram of mean, standard deviations and skews of the sampled stocks returns

Interestingly, changes in the means of the simulated prices for changing the volatility parameter σ of the simulation correspond almost exactly. This can only be the case, if the returns selected for the price simulation are mostly positive ones. This confirms the findings of negative return skewness and positive mean returns from section 3. Only for 30 of all 448 simulated stocks the simulated prices decreased, for all scenarios.

Table 2: Summary statistic of the price simulation

scenario	average price increase	$\Delta\%$ to 1	σ	μ
1	2.72 %		1	0
2	2.99 %	9.93%	1.1	0
3	2.45 %	-9.93%	0.9	0
4	2.98 %	9.56%	1	0.1
5	2.46 %	-9.56%	1	-0.1

Parameters σ and μ control mean and volatility of the returns according to equation 1

4.2 Simulated Option Prices

Put prices were on average smaller than call prices, also confirming the findings from section 3, that positive mean returns and negative skewness lead to a divergence of call from put prices (see table 3). Taking a cursory look at the option price changes at this condensed level reveals relatively small changes with respect to changes in the mean and volatility of the returns. Despite this, the direction of change corresponds to the hypotheses: an increase of return means (scenario 4) leads to an increase in call prices and a decrease in put prices, vice versa for a decrease of return means (scenario 5). This corresponds to the theoretical argumentation, that states that higher return means lead to higher stock prices, which increases call payoff and decreases put payoff, given a fixed strike price.

In the light of the findings of, on average, positive return means and negative return skewness in the stock sample, the changes in volatility (scenario 2 and 3), which signs correspond

Table 3: Price changes of options

scenario	call	put	Δ call	Δ put	σ	μ
1	26.32	23.66			1	0
2	26.55	23.64	0.01 %	-0.001 %	1.1	0
3	26.09	23.70	-0.02 %	0.002 %	0.9	0
4	26.45	23.55	0.01 %	-0.01 %	1	0.1
5	26.18	23.78	-0.01 %	0.01 %	1	-0.1

Parameters σ and μ control mean and volatility of the returns according to equation 1

to scenarios 4 and 5, are to be expected. Still, this would directly contradict hypothesis 2, that states that option prices both ceteris paribus increase with an increase in volatility, although the magnitude of the price decrease of puts is very small.

Taking a deeper look, the determination of the exact relationship of return mean and volatility on option prices is of interest. As already observed, the level of mean returns has influences on the option prices, but also, more importantly, on how the volatility influences the option prices. To assess these relationships, pearsons correlation coefficients are calculated (see table 4). The relationship of return means on the mean of the simulated prices is straightforward: calls are positively, puts negatively correlated with return means, all significant on a 0.1% level. Increasing the volatility (scenario 1) seems to lessen the magnitude of negative correlation, as well as a decrease in mean returns(scenario 5). Overall, hypothesis 1 gets confirmed by this result.

Table 4: Correlations of mean and volatility of the underlying stocks with the means of the simulated option prices

scenario	call	pvalue	put	pvalue
1	0.96	<0.001	-0.54	<0.001
2	0.95	<0.001	-0.47	<0.001
3	0.96	<0.001	-0.62	<0.001
4	0.96	<0.001	-0.61	<0.001
5	0.95	<0.001	-0.46	<0.001

(a) Correlation of the option prices with return means

scenario	call	pvalue	put	pvalue
1	0.85	<0.001	0.06	0.180
2	0.86	<0.001	0.15	<0.001
3	0.85	<0.001	-0.03	0.560
4	0.85	<0.001	-0.01	0.770
5	0.86	<0.001	0.16	<0.001

(b) Correlation of the option prices with return volatility

The means of the call-prices in the sample show a strong positive correlation with stock return volatility which is statistically significant at the 0.1% level. For puts, only in two scenarios a significant positive relation with return volatility is present: for increased volatility (scenario 2) and decreased mean (scenario 5). This mixed evidence leads to the conclusion, that the relationship of volatility and option prices is not exclusive. One explanation is of course, that when volatility increases because of more and higher positive returns, the return and price distribution is not symmetrical, or becomes more asymmetric.

5 Conclusion

In this paper, a simulation study was conducted in order to assess the relationship of stock returns and european option prices. The aim was to identify the determinants of option prices, when structural and institutional factors are left aside. The simulation study used a sample of the S&P500 stocks and simulated future stock prices by sampling returns from these stocks. Additional, the volatility and the mean of the sampled returns was altered in different scenarios to analyse the ceteris paribus effects of such changes.

The results confirmed hypothesis 1. Higher returns ceteris paribus lead to higher call and lower put prices. For a trader, this simply confirms that for stocks with high average returns, i.e. profitable stocks, calls are more profitable.

For hypothesis 2 only mixed evidence was found. Instead of monotonically increasing option prices, only call prices increased with increasing return volatility. Put prices only did so in certain circumstances, e.g. when the volatility and the mean of the returns was increased.

These mixed results might be due to the simulation methodology or the stock sample. The sample exhibited stocks with high average returns and negatively skewed returns. But the distribution of the returns has a strong influence on the simulated prices. In this case, simulated prices tended to increase rather than decrease. This could have been countered by taking another, more balanced stock sample, or by standardising the returns previous to sampling. Although this would have altered the original data, it would shed some light on the relationship of stock returns and option prices. Another approach would be to assess whether the correlations of return mean and volatility changes with their magnitude or sign, or what effect the observed skewness has on the returns.

As a conclusion it can be said, that the obvious relationship of return means and option prices could be confirmed. The relationship of return volatility and option prices depends on the distribution, or symmetry of the returns and without further assumptions about this distribution no exact relationship can be specified.

References

Bali, Turan G. and Armen Hovakimian (2009). "Volatility Spreads and Expected Stock Returns". In: *Management Science* 55.11, pp. 1797–1812.

Beckers, Stan (1981). "Standard Deviations Implied in Option Prices as Predictors of Future Stock Price Variability". In: *Journal of Banking & Finance* 5, pp. 363–381.

Black, Fischer and Myron Scholes (1972). "The Valuation of Option Contracts and a Test of Market Efficiency". In: *The Journal of Finance* 27.2, pp. 399–417.

Cao, Jie and Bing Han (2013). "Cross section of option returns and idiosyncratic stock volatility". In: *Journal of Financial Economics* 108, pp. 231–249.

Futures Industries Association (2018). *Number of futures and options contracts traded worldwide from 2013 to 2017 (in billions). In Statista - The Statistics Portal.* URL: https://www.statista.com/statistics/377025/global-futures-and-options-volume/ (visited on 06/12/2018).

Gurdip Bakshi, Charles Cao and Zhiwo Chen (2000). "Do Call Prices and the Underlying Stock Always Move in the Same Direction?" In: *The Review of Financial Studies* 13.3, pp. 549–584.

Johnson, R. Stafford, Richard A. Zuber, and John M. Gandar (2007). "Pricing Stock Options uder Expected Increasing and Decreasing Price Cases". In: *Quarterly Journal of Business and Economics* 46.4, pp. 63–90.

Latane, Henry A. and Richard J. Rendleman (1976). "Standard Deviations Implied in Option Prices as Predictors of Future Stock Price Variability". In: *The Journal of Finance* 31.2, pp. 369–381.

Lin, Tse-Chun and Xiaolong Lu (2015). "Why do option prices predict stock returns? Evidence from analyst tipping". In: *Journal of Banking & Finance* 52, pp. 369–381.

Pan, J. and A. Poteshman (2006). "The information in option volume for future stock prices". In: *The Review of Financial Studies* 19, pp. 871–908.

Picardo, Elvis (2018). *Five Advantages of Futures Over Options.* URL: https://www.investopedia.com/articles/active-trading/020216/five-advantages-futures-over-options.asp.

6 Appendix

Table 5: Summary statistics of the returns of all stock in the sample

n	stock	min	max	mean	sd	skew
1	AMZN	-75.35	128.52	0.62	9.26	0.84
2	GOOGL	-62.39	97.84	0.32	8.16	0.24
3	GOOG	-56.10	93.08	0.32	8.05	0.29
4	AZO	-81.43	43.92	0.21	6.62	-1.86
5	MTD	-40.96	29.03	0.18	4.10	-0.74
6	NFLX	-19.66	28.28	0.14	2.36	1.64
7	BLK	-24.61	23.66	0.14	4.30	-0.25
8	ISRG	-26.93	35.58	0.14	3.34	0.36
9	ABMD	-28.18	33.43	0.14	2.00	2.01
10	CMG	-86.88	82.98	0.13	7.86	-0.05
11	ALGN	-28.27	32.96	0.13	2.05	0.11
12	SHW	-29.74	21.27	0.13	2.73	-0.81
13	EQIX	-29.77	21.28	0.13	3.37	-0.87
14	TDG	-23.02	20.07	0.12	2.14	-1.23
15	BA	-19.83	20.55	0.12	2.01	0.31
16	REGN	-36.69	50.65	0.11	6.38	0.60
17	NOC	-14.77	12.12	0.11	1.75	-0.24
18	SIVB	-14.37	48.24	0.10	2.43	2.95
19	HUM	-17.04	35.53	0.10	2.15	1.46
20	ORLY	-41.64	29.73	0.10	2.56	-1.26
21	ULTA	-24.24	28.23	0.09	2.62	0.76
22	IPGP	-23.33	20.26	0.09	2.03	-0.46
23	ROP	-18.42	9.60	0.09	1.75	-0.76
24	LMT	-21.97	16.36	0.09	1.85	-0.94
25	NVDA	-19.80	20.07	0.09	1.82	0.40
26	ILMN	-45.86	25.55	0.09	3.01	-2.16
27	GWW	-24.65	42.12	0.09	2.80	1.27
28	BIIB	-85.02	42.33	0.09	4.91	-1.64
29	UNH	-11.78	10.58	0.08	1.32	0.00
30	STZ	-12.43	11.48	0.08	1.29	0.24
31	ADBE	-15.11	18.73	0.08	1.37	0.83
32	SPGI	-10.91	13.53	0.07	1.13	-0.05
33	COO	-14.65	18.53	0.07	1.90	-0.08
34	MA	-8.10	6.96	0.07	1.00	-0.16
35	AAPL	-7.22	7.80	0.07	1.24	0.08

Continued on next page

Table 5 – continued from previous page

n	stock	min	max	mean	sd	skew
36	IDXX	-13.75	16.42	0.07	1.33	0.60
37	INTU	-13.23	9.70	0.07	1.12	-0.09
38	ANTM	-13.49	13.79	0.07	1.64	-0.09
39	FDX	-12.75	16.77	0.07	1.94	0.04
40	HD	-10.74	8.28	0.07	1.05	-0.58
41	BDX	-12.21	15.80	0.06	1.39	-0.00
42	FFIV	-29.63	15.04	0.06	2.23	-1.17
43	COST	-12.80	7.22	0.06	1.27	-0.64
44	MMM	-14.65	12.87	0.06	1.41	-1.18
45	LRCX	-18.30	14.57	0.06	1.72	-0.64
46	PSA	-11.34	10.36	0.06	1.97	-0.25
47	RE	-16.91	16.71	0.06	1.80	0.38
48	AMGN	-14.65	8.20	0.06	1.68	-0.28
49	ADS	-47.02	23.95	0.06	3.07	-1.67
50	URI	-11.78	12.99	0.06	1.69	-0.61
51	ESS	-12.23	12.63	0.06	2.13	-0.19
52	CTAS	-10.18	11.52	0.06	0.92	1.12
53	RTN	-9.33	9.92	0.06	1.13	-0.20
54	MCO	-7.82	6.60	0.06	1.09	-0.52
55	CME	-7.93	6.78	0.05	1.06	-0.03
56	WAT	-19.15	11.19	0.05	1.65	-1.27
57	MHK	-12.40	13.77	0.05	2.15	-0.25
58	SBAC	-9.53	9.89	0.05	1.24	-0.45
59	V	-5.77	5.86	0.05	0.72	-0.13
60	RHT	-11.08	10.04	0.05	1.14	0.01
61	MLM	-14.34	23.05	0.05	2.48	0.44
62	UNP	-7.51	6.94	0.05	1.05	-0.15
63	ACN	-11.70	6.32	0.05	1.02	-1.01
64	ROK	-9.95	13.63	0.05	1.50	-0.03
65	SYK	-7.83	10.85	0.05	1.03	-0.19
66	AET	-7.83	18.38	0.05	1.25	1.02
67	PVH	-10.53	18.35	0.05	1.72	0.32
68	ANSS	-7.33	13.08	0.05	1.17	0.33
69	AGN	-40.11	21.23	0.05	3.00	-0.63
70	PXD	-17.57	19.33	0.05	2.87	-0.07
71	NEE	-7.26	4.56	0.05	0.90	-0.09
72	LLL	-13.50	10.49	0.05	1.40	-0.62
73	CI	-22.24	16.11	0.05	1.56	-1.37

Continued on next page

Table 5 – continued from previous page

n	stock	min	max	mean	sd	skew
74	VRTX	-11.10	32.73	0.05	2.23	3.10
75	MCD	-7.38	9.08	0.05	0.95	0.23
76	MSCI	-9.17	7.77	0.05	0.89	-0.15
77	EL	-12.31	10.23	0.05	0.94	0.19
78	EW	-19.43	15.16	0.05	1.19	-1.38
79	ANDV	-11.97	15.87	0.05	1.25	0.32
80	GD	-10.45	11.74	0.05	1.37	-0.05
81	WYNN	-20.40	15.48	0.05	2.65	-0.16
82	SNA	-12.94	9.63	0.04	1.39	-0.24
83	CNC	-12.75	7.28	0.04	0.96	-1.15
84	PKG	-7.28	5.75	0.04	0.86	-0.35
85	IT	-11.23	7.83	0.04	0.97	-0.76
86	ITW	-10.19	4.80	0.04	0.99	-1.33
87	AVB	-8.60	7.49	0.04	1.73	-0.22
88	NSC	-6.51	10.93	0.04	1.25	0.20
89	SPG	-9.75	8.95	0.04	1.74	-0.37
90	LH	-11.95	6.74	0.04	1.32	-0.77
91	PNC	-12.91	7.17	0.04	1.33	-0.46
92	CRM	-8.69	7.76	0.04	1.04	0.05
93	HON	-8.36	5.30	0.04	0.93	-0.43
94	ADSK	-20.61	17.83	0.04	1.22	-0.26
95	PH	-8.57	6.73	0.04	1.52	-0.31
96	AAP	-29.89	21.37	0.04	1.96	-0.81
97	WHR	-18.84	13.71	0.04	2.22	-0.79
98	HRS	-8.02	9.05	0.04	0.93	-0.19
99	SWK	-11.59	7.46	0.04	1.19	-0.65
100	ADP	-6.33	9.45	0.04	0.77	-0.13
101	ALXN	-16.99	28.27	0.04	2.59	0.47
102	CXO	-16.90	15.69	0.04	2.25	-0.31
103	TIF	-13.46	23.81	0.04	1.26	2.13
104	IFF	-15.26	7.31	0.04	1.13	-1.97
105	JBHT	-5.21	6.97	0.04	0.93	-0.01
106	MTB	-9.31	9.39	0.04	1.58	-0.25
107	EXPE	-23.38	13.46	0.04	1.66	-1.76
108	CAT	-9.55	7.44	0.04	1.34	-0.36
109	SWKS	-5.95	10.03	0.04	1.21	0.07
110	BRK-B	-12.32	8.90	0.04	1.39	-0.16
111	GPN	-5.73	6.40	0.04	0.77	0.03

Continued on next page

Table 5 – continued from previous page

n	stock	min	max	mean	sd	skew
112	CB	-7.09	5.88	0.04	1.00	-0.24
113	DPS	-5.30	21.32	0.04	0.75	8.90
114	VRSN	-7.21	5.76	0.04	0.87	-0.51
115	AMT	-6.51	7.98	0.04	1.02	-0.23
116	MAR	-6.32	6.04	0.04	0.89	-0.24
117	TRV	-7.05	7.19	0.04	0.96	-0.43
118	AON	-5.22	4.00	0.04	0.89	-0.39
119	APD	-7.13	7.53	0.04	1.27	-0.00
120	MCK	-35.86	11.44	0.04	2.02	-2.60
121	ECL	-7.72	5.78	0.04	0.99	-0.48
122	RCL	-12.11	7.70	0.03	1.16	-0.39
123	MSFT	-4.56	6.57	0.03	0.61	0.41
124	CLX	-9.34	6.03	0.03	0.93	-0.81
125	CMI	-10.14	8.92	0.03	1.77	-0.38
126	EFX	-19.29	6.98	0.03	1.08	-4.03
127	DXC	-9.81	13.11	0.03	0.66	4.83
128	TWX	-10.15	11.23	0.03	0.80	-0.24
129	TXN	-10.07	6.17	0.03	0.72	-0.91
130	UHS	-14.93	10.00	0.03	1.41	-1.14
131	MCHP	-8.94	4.39	0.03	0.73	-1.11
132	WLTW	-11.90	8.36	0.03	1.39	-0.73
133	COL	-7.13	7.99	0.03	0.90	0.13
134	FRT	-9.29	7.92	0.03	1.34	-0.16
135	AVY	-4.65	6.45	0.03	0.75	-0.00
136	AWK	-3.87	3.30	0.03	0.50	-0.64
137	MKC	-5.00	5.12	0.03	0.71	-0.40
138	SRE	-5.49	4.13	0.03	0.86	-0.62
139	TTWO	-13.68	11.26	0.03	0.86	-0.25
140	AYI	-34.69	29.67	0.03	2.61	-1.57
141	RJF	-6.43	6.53	0.03	0.85	-0.43
142	DLTR	-15.11	10.01	0.03	0.99	-2.40
143	EMN	-6.51	5.78	0.03	0.91	-0.21
144	ABC	-10.05	8.25	0.03	0.90	-1.05
145	PX	-5.95	6.21	0.03	1.26	-0.01
146	RMD	-9.29	12.75	0.03	0.78	0.55
147	RL	-29.13	16.72	0.03	2.18	-1.23
148	UPS	-10.19	4.58	0.03	0.92	-1.00
149	ADI	-5.07	5.51	0.03	0.75	0.06

Continued on next page

Table 5 – continued from previous page

n	stock	min	max	mean	sd	skew
150	KLAC	-7.54	9.39	0.03	0.95	-0.55
151	JNJ	-7.19	5.05	0.03	0.80	-0.49
152	CTXS	-7.84	8.86	0.03	1.08	0.19
153	VAR	-9.38	13.96	0.03	1.02	0.40
154	DHR	-5.47	27.08	0.03	0.75	18.84
155	MSI	-5.76	4.71	0.03	0.78	-0.05
156	DIS	-10.76	6.88	0.03	0.88	-0.91
157	JPM	-5.76	5.37	0.03	0.94	-0.14
158	NKTR	-7.57	18.32	0.03	0.87	5.13
159	TJX	-4.66	5.35	0.03	0.65	0.16
160	UTX	-7.29	5.13	0.03	1.04	-0.42
161	VFC	-9.19	3.89	0.03	0.64	-2.29
162	DLR	-8.00	5.29	0.03	0.98	-0.71
163	CCI	-5.17	5.15	0.03	0.79	-0.33
164	TROW	-8.28	4.71	0.03	1.03	-0.41
165	EXR	-5.26	3.32	0.03	0.66	-0.56
166	LOW	-6.17	8.94	0.03	0.77	0.47
167	FIS	-8.69	5.45	0.03	0.64	-0.71
168	TSCO	-13.74	9.25	0.03	0.92	-0.94
169	DE	-7.93	10.01	0.03	1.30	0.06
170	DRI	-7.32	6.74	0.03	0.72	-0.18
171	EA	-6.52	12.15	0.03	1.03	0.87
172	VLO	-5.59	4.72	0.03	0.82	-0.37
173	APH	-3.88	3.53	0.03	0.56	-0.42
174	TSS	-6.67	3.85	0.03	0.52	-1.32
175	SJM	-12.05	10.01	0.03	1.08	-0.56
176	DTE	-3.78	2.90	0.03	0.64	-0.44
177	ROST	-5.61	6.51	0.03	0.60	0.09
178	GS	-21.14	19.57	0.03	2.91	-0.29
179	CMA	-4.45	4.64	0.03	0.84	-0.31
180	GILD	-14.38	5.47	0.02	1.08	-1.49
181	IR	-4.66	4.75	0.02	0.73	-0.39
182	KMX	-5.01	7.47	0.02	0.83	0.41
183	PKI	-4.00	4.14	0.02	0.57	-0.39
184	YUM	-10.55	4.78	0.02	0.68	-1.89
185	COF	-11.04	6.81	0.02	1.12	-0.53
186	NTRS	-12.12	11.02	0.02	1.16	-0.51
187	HSIC	-8.07	4.72	0.02	0.73	-1.42

Continued on next page

Table 5 – continued from previous page

n	stock	min	max	mean	sd	skew
188	WDC	-8.44	9.73	0.02	1.18	-0.29
189	CINF	-4.89	3.23	0.02	0.55	-0.87
190	WEC	-2.26	1.57	0.02	0.40	-0.66
191	DAL	-3.09	3.14	0.02	0.60	-0.19
192	RHI	-5.23	3.44	0.02	0.63	-0.92
193	O	-3.09	3.02	0.02	0.52	-0.35
194	MO	-6.73	2.14	0.02	0.43	-2.20
195	PNW	-2.91	3.38	0.02	0.54	-0.37
196	CTSH	-7.19	3.99	0.02	0.75	-0.90
197	MU	-4.98	4.78	0.02	0.57	-0.25
198	AXP	-7.30	7.22	0.02	0.92	-0.32
199	SNPS	-4.29	4.40	0.02	0.54	-0.72
200	MMC	-3.08	3.05	0.02	0.49	-0.32
201	KSU	-16.75	5.79	0.02	1.39	-1.28
202	CSX	-4.35	8.44	0.02	0.50	1.83
203	AAL	-4.66	3.45	0.02	0.67	-0.28
204	PM	-15.80	5.95	0.02	0.83	-2.84
205	STX	-8.01	4.86	0.02	0.69	-1.42
206	TEL	-5.46	3.54	0.02	0.69	-0.53
207	EOG	-7.16	9.98	0.02	1.40	0.05
208	IBM	-14.26	12.60	0.02	1.70	-0.65
209	FISV	-3.72	2.28	0.02	0.38	-0.63
210	ATVI	-3.94	7.42	0.02	0.56	0.74
211	PRU	-7.66	10.32	0.02	1.30	-0.28
212	ICE	-3.70	4.04	0.02	0.56	-0.03
213	ABT	-3.57	2.48	0.02	0.42	-0.90
214	PRGO	-21.53	29.59	0.02	1.96	0.45
215	DFS	-4.19	4.10	0.02	0.63	-0.42
216	MNST	-9.15	7.28	0.02	0.60	0.08
217	CVX	-6.86	8.42	0.02	1.21	-0.18
218	HSY	-11.51	15.57	0.02	0.87	1.03
219	NTAP	-5.31	7.24	0.02	0.71	0.31
220	OKE	-3.39	7.41	0.02	0.59	0.42
221	INTC	-3.14	4.72	0.02	0.42	0.64
222	NDAQ	-4.50	5.16	0.02	0.67	0.18
223	EQR	-4.49	5.95	0.02	0.72	-0.01
224	AEP	-2.46	2.43	0.02	0.47	-0.33
225	PAYX	-2.85	3.15	0.02	0.44	-0.20

Continued on next page

Table 5 – continued from previous page

n	stock	min	max	mean	sd	skew
226	SYY	-3.68	4.52	0.02	0.40	0.54
227	WMT	-10.54	9.62	0.02	0.75	-0.57
228	ETN	-5.45	4.78	0.02	0.76	-0.29
229	ESRX	-7.73	6.30	0.02	0.97	-0.35
230	CELG	-19.57	11.62	0.02	1.52	-1.08
231	WM	-4.73	3.74	0.02	0.45	-0.36
232	GPC	-8.14	5.12	0.02	0.83	-0.71
233	TMK	-4.24	3.20	0.02	0.55	-0.53
234	LLY	-7.68	5.11	0.02	0.73	-0.62
235	AJG	-3.69	4.78	0.02	0.40	0.27
236	HAS	-10.68	11.33	0.02	0.89	0.36
237	ALB	-11.06	8.89	0.02	1.22	-0.85
238	ALK	-10.32	5.21	0.02	0.87	-0.88
239	ALL	-6.74	4.16	0.02	0.69	-1.19
240	DOV	-4.31	4.33	0.02	0.71	-0.25
241	AME	-4.18	2.59	0.02	0.55	-0.47
242	AMG	-18.31	15.76	0.02	2.63	-0.20
243	MAA	-5.55	5.05	0.02	0.89	-0.39
244	UAL	-8.92	5.10	0.02	1.02	-0.50
245	NKE	-4.03	5.76	0.02	0.55	0.77
246	CERN	-6.01	4.91	0.02	0.72	-0.14
247	INCY	-19.05	13.30	0.02	1.82	-0.49
248	BXP	-11.01	10.97	0.02	1.53	-0.31
249	PEP	-5.48	3.22	0.02	0.70	-0.47
250	XLNX	-6.23	4.30	0.02	0.64	-0.76
251	ED	-3.08	2.25	0.02	0.52	-0.50
252	VMC	-7.55	11.65	0.02	1.47	0.28
253	AOS	-3.07	2.42	0.02	0.40	-0.71
254	FMC	-4.70	8.03	0.02	0.88	0.28
255	TSN	-9.48	4.97	0.02	0.63	-1.86
256	ES	-2.88	3.38	0.02	0.42	-0.36
257	FL	-13.00	9.35	0.02	0.81	-1.57
258	PGR	-2.33	3.08	0.02	0.33	0.13
259	SBUX	-5.39	2.74	0.02	0.47	-0.86
260	MDT	-6.75	3.74	0.02	0.70	-0.45
261	ZBH	-16.94	10.18	0.02	1.21	-1.10
262	ARE	-9.99	7.32	0.02	1.23	-0.59
263	DUK	-3.79	4.09	0.02	0.59	-0.39

Continued on next page

Table 5 – continued from previous page

n	stock	min	max	mean	sd	skew
264	BAX	-3.16	3.46	0.02	0.44	-0.41
265	DVA	-5.93	8.27	0.02	0.76	0.07
266	BF-B	-3.08	3.19	0.02	0.35	-0.11
267	LUV	-4.63	4.40	0.02	0.54	-0.50
268	KMB	-6.56	5.22	0.02	0.87	-0.48
269	BBY	-9.55	10.51	0.01	0.82	-0.24
270	HP	-6.96	7.53	0.01	1.24	-0.22
271	FOX	-2.16	2.18	0.01	0.36	-0.04
272	CMCSA	-2.90	1.87	0.01	0.30	-0.88
273	CMS	-1.57	1.19	0.01	0.28	-0.55
274	IP	-3.52	2.47	0.01	0.57	-0.44
275	SCHW	-3.48	3.78	0.01	0.52	-0.18
276	CDNS	-3.16	3.35	0.01	0.30	-0.27
277	WBA	-9.67	5.38	0.01	0.85	-0.90
278	REG	-5.40	5.32	0.01	0.81	-0.34
279	CNP	-1.06	1.26	0.01	0.21	-0.17
280	PLD	-4.02	3.56	0.01	0.65	-0.56
281	COP	-4.28	4.16	0.01	0.80	-0.13
282	KO	-2.31	1.93	0.01	0.31	-0.41
283	KR	-5.60	2.21	0.01	0.35	-2.34
284	LB	-8.56	4.37	0.01	0.83	-1.75
285	EIX	-10.07	3.00	0.01	0.61	-2.21
286	A	-6.71	2.99	0.01	0.59	-0.85
287	D	-4.16	2.37	0.01	0.54	-0.52
288	VTR	-16.07	4.81	0.01	0.88	-2.65
289	TAP	-10.97	9.82	0.01	0.90	-0.04
290	K	-4.44	3.84	0.01	0.61	-0.28
291	AMAT	-4.43	3.08	0.01	0.48	-0.98
292	M	-5.77	5.24	0.01	0.63	-0.41
293	PNR	-3.28	3.38	0.01	0.49	-0.29
294	MS	-5.98	7.24	0.01	0.71	-0.14
295	XOM	-7.55	8.01	0.01	0.96	-0.04
296	WFC	-5.87	5.23	0.01	0.68	0.05
297	NI	-0.97	0.86	0.01	0.16	-0.29
298	ORCL	-4.88	3.97	0.01	0.49	-0.64
299	FOXA	-2.32	2.47	0.01	0.38	-0.04
300	KSS	-9.08	5.54	0.01	0.89	-1.24
301	STI	-9.93	6.63	0.01	0.83	-0.59

Continued on next page

Table 5 – continued from previous page

n	stock	min	max	mean	sd	skew
302	EMR	-3.97	3.75	0.01	0.70	-0.11
303	EBAY	-3.50	5.61	0.01	0.39	0.88
304	PG	-4.11	4.34	0.01	0.64	-0.30
305	UNM	-8.12	2.92	0.01	0.53	-2.05
306	STT	-18.71	11.15	0.01	1.26	-1.71
307	QCOM	-8.30	6.78	0.01	0.88	-0.92
308	LEG	-2.94	3.12	0.01	0.42	-0.50
309	LEN	-3.28	5.73	0.01	0.70	0.05
310	FITB	-5.83	2.61	0.01	0.37	-1.84
311	HRL	-3.18	2.80	0.01	0.29	-0.74
312	FAST	-3.91	3.66	0.01	0.59	-0.40
313	BLL	-2.01	4.11	0.01	0.34	0.86
314	GIS	-4.37	3.23	0.01	0.45	-0.79
315	CVS	-9.48	4.69	0.01	0.82	-1.14
316	TGT	-7.75	4.98	0.01	0.84	-0.64
317	ADM	-3.91	3.02	0.01	0.54	-0.58
318	BMY	-11.49	4.42	0.01	0.66	-2.69
319	SO	-1.95	2.22	0.01	0.34	-0.14
320	DHI	-2.93	2.74	0.01	0.46	-0.17
321	MRK	-3.66	5.66	0.01	0.54	0.44
322	USB	-2.82	3.26	0.01	0.53	-0.14
323	OMC	-5.41	3.17	0.01	0.70	-0.55
324	AFL	-5.19	3.01	0.01	0.44	-1.06
325	DWDP	-3.02	5.59	0.01	0.64	0.08
326	CAG	-2.83	3.06	0.01	0.29	-0.06
327	CAH	-13.85	3.82	0.01	0.84	-3.12
328	EXPD	-5.21	5.58	0.01	0.70	0.12
329	VZ	-2.45	3.29	0.01	0.40	0.03
330	LKQ	-7.17	3.04	0.01	0.40	-2.45
331	CBS	-3.51	4.41	0.01	0.66	0.15
332	XL	-3.60	12.52	0.01	0.51	5.66
333	CCL	-3.86	3.31	0.01	0.66	-0.33
334	AIV	-6.62	2.82	0.01	0.48	-1.56
335	AIZ	-9.67	6.19	0.01	0.90	-0.95
336	LNC	-8.41	8.00	0.01	0.92	-0.70
337	BSX	-2.12	2.20	0.01	0.26	0.40
338	ETFC	-8.50	6.40	0.01	0.75	-0.75
339	SEE	-4.19	4.15	0.01	0.51	-0.51

Continued on next page

Table 5 – continued from previous page

n	stock	min	max	mean	sd	skew
340	LNT	-1.62	1.34	0.01	0.25	-0.55
341	GRMN	-6.18	5.07	0.01	0.62	-0.38
342	CHRW	-7.71	3.74	0.01	0.93	-1.07
343	MYL	-9.57	8.79	0.01	0.78	-0.25
344	PCG	-6.78	4.01	0.01	0.55	-1.88
345	BK	-8.21	5.37	0.01	0.68	-0.43
346	BWA	-3.81	3.69	0.01	0.71	-0.29
347	UAA	-7.45	7.74	0.01	0.56	-0.16
348	TPR	-9.20	4.25	0.01	0.80	-1.52
349	CA	-3.44	4.09	0.01	0.35	-0.25
350	MAC	-5.04	5.71	0.01	0.82	-0.16
351	CF	-4.38	5.48	0.01	0.68	-0.17
352	JWN	-8.73	7.55	0.01	0.83	-0.55
353	PCAR	-4.47	3.17	0.01	0.79	-0.33
354	CL	-3.73	4.02	0.01	0.54	-0.23
355	XEC	-10.49	13.82	0.01	2.00	0.12
356	HOLX	-4.38	2.72	0.01	0.47	-1.11
357	CHD	-3.04	2.06	0.01	0.34	-0.83
358	MAS	-3.29	2.39	0.01	0.37	-0.57
359	PEG	-2.04	2.86	0.01	0.41	-0.10
360	FLIR	-4.28	4.16	0.01	0.55	-0.08
361	XEL	-1.83	1.14	0.01	0.28	-0.55
362	DRE	-1.84	1.41	0.01	0.28	-0.49
363	PFE	-1.92	2.00	0.01	0.27	0.09
364	PFG	-5.89	6.47	0.01	0.77	-0.64
365	IPG	-3.29	2.23	0.01	0.25	-0.85
366	MDLZ	-2.61	2.69	0.01	0.40	0.06
367	AKAM	-12.64	9.76	0.01	1.08	-0.85
368	VNO	-7.27	6.20	0.01	0.94	-0.28
369	PHM	-2.15	1.81	0.01	0.37	-0.25
370	SLG	-14.13	6.67	0.01	1.35	-0.81
371	IRM	-3.61	4.21	0.01	0.38	-0.19
372	ZION	-9.11	8.64	0.01	0.83	-0.13
373	CSCO	-3.23	2.28	0.01	0.36	-0.55
374	OXY	-8.70	6.80	0.01	1.20	-0.14
375	BBT	-6.97	5.01	0.01	0.57	-0.57
376	JCI	-3.12	3.11	0.01	0.38	-0.21
377	NRG	-3.31	5.12	-0.00	0.52	0.47

Continued on next page

Table 5 – continued from previous page

n	stock	min	max	mean	sd	skew
378	TXT	-5.02	4.68	0.00	0.68	-0.29
379	COG	-3.14	2.91	0.00	0.49	0.24
380	BEN	-3.65	3.78	0.00	0.59	-0.31
381	XRAY	-5.15	3.63	0.00	0.62	-0.51
382	CPB	-4.85	3.49	0.00	0.49	-1.34
383	IVZ	-3.68	2.26	0.00	0.47	-0.48
384	FTI	-4.21	3.16	0.00	0.70	-0.20
385	F	-1.96	0.80	0.00	0.19	-0.76
386	L	-5.74	5.79	0.00	0.60	-0.72
387	NUE	-7.54	6.30	0.00	0.88	-0.34
388	SRCL	-28.73	6.74	0.00	1.46	-6.21
389	T	-2.27	2.17	0.00	0.31	-0.18
390	HOG	-7.19	8.45	0.00	0.81	-0.15
391	HBAN	-2.35	2.70	0.00	0.21	0.85
392	PBCT	-2.22	1.91	0.00	0.20	-0.45
393	DISCA	-3.99	2.53	0.00	0.47	-0.37
394	HPQ	-1.97	1.44	0.00	0.25	-0.44
395	NWL	-10.72	5.35	0.00	0.52	-3.80
396	GGP	-4.13	3.13	-0.00	0.33	-1.28
397	CTL	-6.06	2.44	0.00	0.36	-2.13
398	JNPR	-6.08	3.74	0.00	0.54	-0.71
399	HRB	-4.74	2.96	0.00	0.42	-0.55
400	DISH	-4.29	6.81	0.00	0.78	0.09
401	RF	-4.85	4.38	0.00	0.29	-0.70
402	HST	-1.46	2.59	0.00	0.28	-0.03
403	VIAB	-8.39	4.89	-0.00	0.78	-1.01
404	NBL	-4.43	4.17	-0.00	0.85	-0.10
405	MRO	-3.35	3.05	-0.00	0.49	-0.24
406	AES	-1.48	1.56	-0.00	0.22	0.01
407	WMB	-5.15	10.42	0.00	0.59	2.22
408	GLW	-2.00	1.94	0.00	0.31	-0.37
409	PWR	-7.47	4.40	0.00	0.59	-1.19
410	ETR	-4.08	6.19	0.00	0.79	0.06
411	NEM	-4.17	5.06	-0.00	0.88	0.00
412	WU	-4.31	2.22	0.00	0.30	-1.67
413	WY	-20.04	3.71	-0.00	0.69	-10.22
414	SCG	-4.16	8.50	0.00	0.57	0.63
415	HAL	-5.49	5.16	0.00	0.84	-0.37

Continued on next page

Table 5 – continued from previous page

n	stock	min	max	mean	sd	skew
416	HBI	-4.17	3.80	0.00	0.32	-1.28
417	KEY	-4.06	3.49	0.00	0.29	-1.12
418	AMD	-3.30	1.69	0.00	0.24	-0.85
419	HCP	-4.53	3.53	0.00	0.45	-0.38
420	MAT	-5.35	3.38	0.00	0.41	-1.39
421	KIM	-2.78	2.96	-0.00	0.35	-0.15
422	APC	-9.61	12.07	-0.00	1.52	-0.19
423	FLS	-5.98	7.25	0.00	0.82	-0.36
424	BAC	-7.64	6.23	-0.00	0.54	-1.20
425	SYMC	-9.63	1.87	0.00	0.36	-8.08
426	GE	-1.63	2.46	-0.00	0.29	0.01
427	GT	-3.10	2.63	0.00	0.47	-0.54
428	MET	-6.68	8.14	0.00	0.80	-0.12
429	HIG	-9.90	6.79	-0.00	0.80	-1.21
430	MGM	-6.30	5.41	-0.01	0.61	-0.33
431	JEC	-7.32	7.61	-0.01	1.13	-0.40
432	BHGE	-5.74	5.90	-0.01	0.84	-0.24
433	EQT	-6.56	5.33	-0.01	1.24	-0.09
434	FCX	-5.29	3.53	-0.01	0.73	-0.41
435	NFX	-6.24	6.12	-0.01	1.11	-0.39
436	EXC	-3.89	5.29	-0.01	0.53	-0.03
437	FLR	-13.17	6.49	-0.01	1.23	-0.80
438	FE	-3.37	4.96	-0.01	0.50	-0.05
439	SLB	-10.08	6.63	-0.01	1.30	-0.36
440	NOV	-7.40	6.18	-0.01	1.12	-0.41
441	DVN	-11.10	11.39	-0.02	1.40	-0.20
442	RRC	-7.59	6.54	-0.02	1.34	-0.14
443	ARNC	-6.68	6.01	-0.02	0.76	-0.61
444	HES	-11.93	11.29	-0.02	1.55	-0.66
445	MOS	-23.21	9.93	-0.03	1.43	-2.50
446	APA	-12.93	12.64	-0.03	1.76	-0.27
447	C	-39.85	38.41	-0.06	2.80	-0.27
448	AIG	-112.85	48.91	-0.20	4.92	-9.75

Figure 3: Correlations of mean and volatility of the underlying stocks with the means of the simulated option prices

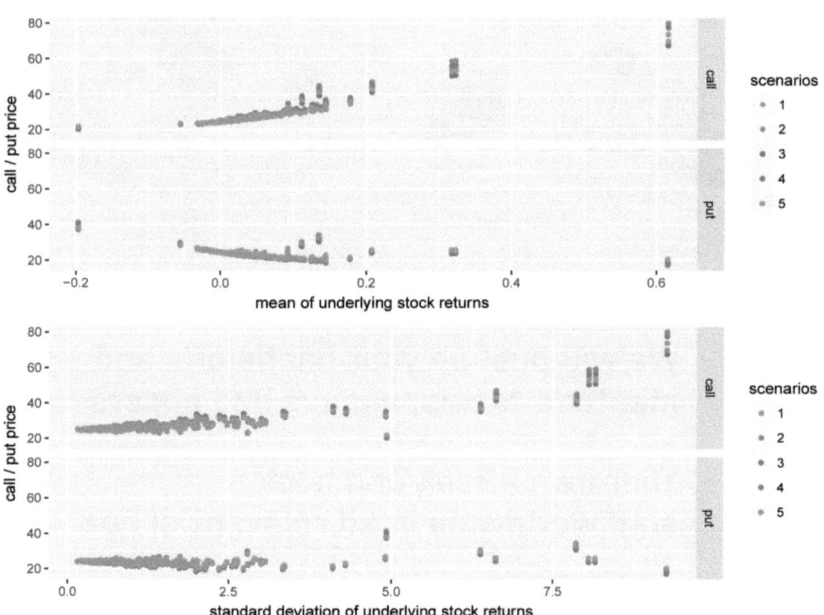

Scenarios: Normal(1), increased / decreased volatility (2/3), increased / decreased mean (4/5)

YOUR KNOWLEDGE HAS VALUE

- We will publish your bachelor's and
  master's thesis, essays and papers

- Your own eBook and book -
  sold worldwide in all relevant shops

- Earn money with each sale

Upload your text at www.GRIN.com
and publish for free